Cynthia Rylant

The Library of Author Biographies™

CYNTHIA RYLANT

Alice B. McGinty

rosen
central™

The Rosen Publishing Group, Inc., New York

Published in 2004 by The Rosen Publishing Group, Inc.
29 East 21st Street, New York, NY 10010

Library of Congress Cataloging-in-Publication Data

McGinty, Alice B., 1963–
Cynthia Rylant/Alice B. McGinty.—1st ed.
    p. cm —(The library of author biographies)
Summary: Discusses the life and work of author Cynthia Rylant, including her writing process and methods, inspirations, a critical discussion of her books, biographical timeline, and awards.
Includes bibliographical references and index.
ISBN 0-8239-4526-X (library binding)
1. Rylant, Cynthia—Juvenile literature. 2. Authors, American—20th century—Biography—Juvenile literature. 3. Children's literature—Authorship—Juvenile literature. [1. Rylant, Cynthia. 2. Authors, American. 3. Women—Biography.] I. Title. II. Series.
PS3568.Y55Z77 2003
813'.54—dc22

                                                            2003012425

Manufactured in the United States of America

Table of Contents

Introduction: One Sunday Morning

It is a sunny morning in Oregon, and Cynthia Rylant feels that certain itch to write. It's been several weeks since she's written, but she grabs her pen and yellow pad of notebook paper and finds a comfortable spot on her front porch swing. Sitting there patiently, she relaxes and daydreams and waits for the words to come. When they do, they flow quickly—so fast that Rylant is only aware of the first few sentences she jots down. An hour later, when her writing is done, Rylant reads what she has written and knows right away whether or not it is good. Usually it is.

Most of Cynthia Rylant's stories come to her on sunny days in that quick, almost mysterious way. During her career as an award-winning children's book author, Cynthia Rylant has written over 130 books. They span a wide age range, including board books and picture books, easy readers, collections of poetry and short stories, and young adult novels. Rylant's picture books include her acclaimed first book, *When I Was Young in the Mountains* (1982). Her easy-reader series feature well-known and much-loved characters such as Henry and Mudge, Mr. Putter and Tabby, and Poppleton the Pig. Her novels, such as the Newbery Award–winning *Missing May* (1992), are renowned as being sensitive, beautifully written, and wise.

Though her writing spans a wide variety of ages and subject matter, there are several themes that are common to Cynthia Rylant's entire body of work. These themes include love and family, loneliness and loss. Rylant explains the reasons for these common themes when she says,

> I think the best writing is that which is most personal, most revealing. Because we all, I think, long mostly for the same things and are afraid mostly of the same things and we all want someone to write about all of this so we don't feel too crazy or alone.[1]

In her life, Rylant has longed for love and family. Though she describes her childhood as a happy one, it was also difficult. As a young girl, she was separated from her father, and for a time, from her mother, too. Rylant believes that the intense feelings of loss and loneliness she experienced then may have provided her with the fuel she needed to become a writer. "They say that to be a writer you must first have an unhappy childhood," Rylant writes in her auto-biography, *But I'll Be Back Again: An Album* (1989). "I don't know if unhappiness is necessary, but I think maybe some children who have suffered a loss too great for words grow up into writers who are always trying to find those words, trying to find a meaning for the way they have lived."[2]

Perhaps this is why the common themes of Rylant's books include the fundamental con-nections between people through family, friendship, and love. Rylant remembers intensely the experiences of her childhood, and it is these connections she longs for most. She remembers what it felt like to be lonely, and to need love, family, and a home, and she knows the joy she found in the love of those around her. It is these basic, deep emotions and the beauty she creates with words that give her books their power and endurance.

"Cynthia Rylant demonstrates a [unique] ability to evoke the strongest of emotions from the simplest of words," states Eden Edwards in the popular reference book *Children's Books and Their Creators*. "She recreates in her characters the unconditional love and acceptance she felt from family and those around her."[3] Rylant's books, for the youngest readers on up, are about making families out of those who are near. They explore relationships, caring, and kindness.

Fortunately, in Rylant's life, many people came together to embrace her along the way. These people and the places that she called home are reflected most strongly in her writing. Cynthia spent much of her childhood living with her grandparents in the Appalachian Mountains of West Virginia. She grew up listening to them tell stories, speaking in the simple, direct, and poetic voice of Appalachia. That voice stayed with Cynthia, and when she later began to write, the poetic language came through.

Rebecca Caudill, a well-known Appalachian author, describes the people of Appalachia in her memoirs. "The people found their pleasures in the simple things of life. They possessed a kind of profound wisdom, characteristic of those who live close to Nature, who walk in step with

Nature's rhythm, and who depend on Nature for life itself."[4]

Cynthia Rylant's books possess that same wisdom—a profound wisdom that she feels is part of the mystery of her writing. It is an insight and depth, however, which Rylant has accumulated over a lifetime of experience. Along with her own experience, she has spent her life observing those around her with a sensitive, watchful eye. Seeing her grandparents overcome the hardships of their lives with grace and dignity led Rylant to develop a strong appreciation and understanding of older people.

Rylant is known for her sympathetic and realistic portrayal of older people in her stories. Many of her books feature those people in our society who quietly stay in the background. In her stories, older folks, homeless people, those with mental disabilities, and quiet, struggling families hidden in rural Appalachia all come alive. Through her writing, Rylant allows them to step forward and show us their inner beauty. Her books sing with the importance of all living things, animals and people young and old.

1 The Early Years

Cynthia Rylant was born on June 6, 1954, on an army base in Hopewell, Virginia. She was named Cynthia Smith by her mother, Leatrel Rylant Smith, and her father, John Tune Smith. John was a sergeant in the United States Army. His job as a soldier took the family to Columbia, South Carolina; Kyoto, Japan; and Peoria, Illinois, during Cynthia's first few years of life. Leatrel took care of Cynthia as the family was transferred from one army base to the next.

Cynthia adored her parents. Her mother was beautiful and caring, and her father was playful and witty. The family had a small dog named Sissy, and Cynthia had an imaginary friend named Gretchen and several stuffed animals. When Cynthia's father made her stuffed animals talk with each other, she was enchanted.

Along with these joyful times at home, however, Cynthia's early years were plagued with unhappy times. Her father's artistic flair led him to become frustrated with army life, which was very rigid. Frequently, he turned to alcohol to help him forget his frustrations. His drunkenness had a devastating effect on the family. He and Leatrel had loud arguments, and their marriage became stormy and difficult. Cynthia would later describe her parents' marriage as an "ongoing cyclone."[1] She remembers this time with much sadness. She felt guilty for the unhappiness at home, and in her innocence, felt that she was the cause of her parents' troubles.

Her parents' marriage became increasingly difficult. Finally, when Cynthia was four years old, her mother could no longer stand living with her alcoholic father. Leatrel and Cynthia fled from their home in Peoria, Illinois, and went to Cool Ridge, West Virginia, to the home where Leatrel had grown up.

Searching

Cynthia barely knew Elda and Ferrell Rylant, her grandparents in West Virginia. Their home was nestled far in the Appalachian Mountains, and she'd visited only one or two times in her life. Cynthia missed her dog, Sissy, and her toys. Most of all, though, Cynthia missed her father and wanted him back. She watched the dirt roads that led to that small white house in Cool Ridge, hoping that any minute, her father might return.

However, her mother knew that the separation from her husband was permanent. After leaving him and the life they had together in the army, she turned to the task of building a new life for herself and Cynthia. She had no formal job training, and she wanted a career that would pay well enough to provide for them. Leatrel made the decision to become a nurse. She was accepted at a good nursing school, but it was far away from Cool Ridge. Because she couldn't take care of her young daughter while studying full-time, Leatrel asked her parents to take care of Cynthia while she attended school.

When Leatrel left for nursing school, her parents' small four-room house in the mountains became her daughter's home. And Cynthia's grandparents stepped in to become parents to the nervous little blond-haired girl with wide blue eyes who had lost a father and a mother, and everything she'd known as home.

A Home in the Mountains

Cynthia's new home was already filled with people, but they all welcomed her. Leatrel was one of six children, and her youngest sister and brother, both in high school, were still living at home. Sue shared her bed with Cynthia and worked hard to keep her giggling every night. Joe, a handsome high school basketball star, was preparing to join the air force after his graduation. Cynthia looked up to him with admiration and liked to think of him as an older brother.

Elda and Ferrell Rylant ran their home with quiet, gentle strength. Ferrell, whom Cynthia called Grandaddy, was a coal miner. He had worked mining coal since he was nine years old, first in rural Alabama where he and Elda had grown up, and then in the mountains of West Virginia where they raised their family. Many of the men in Cool Ridge were coal miners. Their work was hard and their wages were extremely low. Although money was of little importance to the people of this community, poverty left them without many of the luxuries, such as electricity, that were common in other parts of the country. The Rylant home had electricity, but like many other homes in the area, it did not have running water. Cynthia became used to using an outhouse, which they called a johnnyhouse.

Ferrell was injured in a rock fall in the mine shortly after Cynthia came to stay with the family. The injury was permanent and left him unable to work. This left the family with even less money. However, they got by living on food from the government, help from generous neighbors, and their own resourcefulness. The Rylant family raised chickens, grew a big garden, and harvested apples and cherries from trees. Ferrell hunted squirrels for meat.

Elda, Cynthia's Grandmama, made sure everyone was well taken care of. She cooked the squirrel meat and kept the kitchen table covered with good food. She made wonderful pancake breakfasts and suppers of cornbread, beans, and fried okra. Elda was calm, hardworking, and devoted to her family. She shooed rat snakes out of their yard with a hoe, bathed

Cynthia in a tin tub, and warmed her up afterward with hot cocoa. Cynthia was well fed and protected. She felt rich with what she had.

When Cynthia's cousins, Peter and Betty, ages seven and nine, came to live with the Rylant family for a year (their parents had gone to Alaska with the air force) they, too, were welcomed. During that year, the three children often played together. "My cousins and I were always in trouble,"[2] Rylant remembers. Others joined the family from time to time, too, including Cynthia's Auntie Dottie who liked to call Cynthia "Lucy Kate," a nickname Cynthia's mother had also used for her. Most people called Cynthia "Cyndi," however, a name by which her friends continue to know her today.

Though Cynthia missed her parents desperately, she soon became comfortable in her new home. She felt treasured and welcomed by the whole community. A keen observer of people, she remembers the times when neighbors stopped by. "When people stopped by," she later recalled, "we all kind of sat around Grandma's round table in the kitchen and people would just talk. I heard a whole lot of coal camp stories, and a lot of stories about all the trouble people used to get into."[3]

Cynthia spent a lot of time roaming around Cool Ridge, observing those who lived and worked there and listening to their stories. She also played in the wooded mountains surrounding their home. Sometimes she played by herself, enjoying the open spaces and the silence of nature. More often, Cynthia played with her best friend, Cindy Mills. Cindy lived just down the hill on the dirt road and the two girls spent a lot of time together, going back and forth to each other's houses. They played in the mountains, following dirt roads, jumping into a muddy swimming hole, smelling honeysuckle, and rescuing stray dogs and cats that they found. Often they pretended that they were witches, German spies, and bad guys.

When Cynthia started school, her first grade teacher, Mrs. Underwood, helped her feel right at home. She encouraged her students to develop a love for learning, and though the school had no library and few books, Cynthia learned to read. She made friends at school and was happy there.

Visits and Letters

Cynthia was happiest of all when her mother visited the Rylant home during breaks from nursing school. She bubbled over with news, telling her mother about school and friends and all that she'd been doing. These visits never lasted long enough, though. When her mother had to return to school, Cynthia ran to her grandparents' bedroom and cried, feeling the loss all over again. Cynthia often wrote her mother letters asking when she was coming home again. Her mother always wrote back, putting a stick of chewing gum in each letter.

Cynthia missed her father, too. She continued to search for him, keeping an eye on the road, hoping for his return. She bought him gifts, but they sat unopened. When Cynthia had first come to West Virginia, her father had sent her letters. In one, he wrote, "Daddy misses and loves you very much and I think you're the finest little girl in the world. I hope we can see each other before long."[4] However, the letters from her father stopped coming after a while. When Cynthia asked her family where he was, she got no answers. Cynthia sensed their discomfort when she spoke of her father, so she thought she was wrong to ask about him. She stopped asking, but she never stopped waiting for him.

Memories

It is these times in Cool Ridge that Rylant would remember vividly later on in her life. As she would later reflect: "It was hard for me, being away from my parents during that time, and so maybe everything I felt . . . I felt more intensely. And when you write stories, it's always your most intense feelings that come out. At least it's so for me."[5]

Memories of her grandfather coming home from the coal mines would make up the opening lines of her first published book, *When I Was Young in the Mountains* (1982). These lines read, "When I was young in the mountains, Grandfather came home in the evening covered with the black dust of a coal mine. Only his lips were clean, and he used them to kiss the top of my head."[6]

Rylant continues the book with vivid descriptions of scenes from these years, including pumping water from the well, going to church in the schoolhouse, and spending quiet evenings with her grandparents, sitting on the porch swing. Her love for Cool Ridge shines brightly in the ending lines of the book, which read, "When I was young in the mountains, I never wanted to go to the ocean, and I never wanted to go to the desert. I never wanted to go anywhere else in the world, for I was in the mountains. And that was always enough."[7]

2 Beaver

When Cynthia was eight years old, her mother, Leatrel, finished nursing school and returned to Cool Ridge. Leatrel found a job as a nurse, and she and Cynthia moved to the tiny town of Beaver, West Virginia, a twenty-minute drive from Cool Ridge. They would continue to visit Cynthia's grandparents on Sundays.

In Beaver, Leatrel found a place to live, a house by the railroad tracks that had been split into two apartments. Though the floors had cigarette burns, spiders lived in the bathtub, and it looked out at a junkyard, they called it home. The three-room apartment had running water and an indoor bathroom, which Cynthia regarded as a great luxury; no more trips to the johnnyhouse.

Cynthia welcomed her new hometown with the creek and railroad tracks running through it. Beaver offered sidewalks, the first Cynthia had seen, a corner drugstore, and a little market where she could buy grape soda pop. There were many children around with whom Cynthia would spend the rest of her childhood. Cynthia remembers her first week in grade three at Beaver Elementary, where, surrounded by new children, she was terrified. However, the teacher, Miss Evans, helped her feel more comfortable. In fact, she made a lasting impression on Cynthia with an ongoing adventure story she made up and told the class. It starred the members of the class, who explored dangerous places like the African jungles. In one part of the story, Cynthia was saved by a classmate from a rattlesnake bite in the Sahara Desert.

Cynthia wasn't read to very often, and her experience with books was limited, but she retained vivid memories of the stories she was told. Like her previous school, Beaver Elementary had no library and the town of Beaver had no public library. Cynthia did develop a love for comic books, though. With the money she earned collecting pop bottles for recycling, she bought

Archie comics at the corner drugstore. She traded piles of comics with a neighbor, Danny, across their backyard fence. "I read comic books non-stop . . ."[1] she remembers. She would later read her way through popular teen mysteries, the Nancy Drew series, which she bought on Saturday trips to Beckley, West Virginia.

Happy Times

Cynthia was a friendly child and soon made many friends, most of them boys. They rode their bikes, played games in the streets, and went exploring around town. With her mother working long hours as a nurse, Cynthia also became accustomed to being home alone after school and taking care of herself. While she spent some of this time with friends, she also enjoyed being by herself. She would continue to love the quiet and freedom of an empty house as an adult.

Cynthia spent some of her time at home watching television. While the television reception in Cool Ridge had been terrible, in Beaver it was good. When Cynthia was nine years old, she watched a nationwide phenomenon on TV. That phenomenon was the Beatles. On February 9, 1964, Cynthia saw their first nationally televised appearance when they performed on the *Ed Sullivan Show*. She fell immediately and desperately in love with Paul McCartney and became a Beatle-maniac. "I covered my bedroom with their pictures, bought their bubblegum cards with every spare dime, listened to their records nonstop from the time I got home from school to bedtime, and wrote desperate letters to Paul McCartney,"[2] she admits.

While she was waiting for Paul McCartney to respond to her letters, Cynthia became interested in boys a bit closer to home. At age eleven, during a game of spin the bottle at a party, Cynthia experienced a milestone in her young life—her first kiss. Describing it in detail in her autobiography, *But I'll Be Back Again*, she says, "I thought every organ inside my body was going to take flight."[3] Following the kiss and a crush on the boy who had delivered it, Cynthia entered into her junior high school years. During the next few years, Cynthia admits, "I did so much kissing that I barely had time to take a breath."[4] From one boyfriend to the next, Cynthia enjoyed every moment.

> I was a majorette in the tiny junior high band and I loved the rush of junior high football games under bright stadium lights, the big white boots I wore, the pert little velvet uniform. I felt very happy in those three years and though I believe I drove my mother out of her mind, I had the time of my life.[5]

Losses

During Cynthia's junior high years, her father, John, who had made no contact with her for years, began to write to her again. Cynthia embraced this contact with her father, sending him long letters and photographs. In his correspondence, John asked Cynthia to visit him in Florida, where he was living. However, the reunion between them never happened. John became ill and was hospitalized. Many years before, when he was a soldier in the Korean War, John had contracted hepatitis B, a disease that destroys the liver. John's heavy drinking worsened the disease, and it finally took its toll on his body. On June 16, 1967, just after Cynthia's thirteenth birthday, her mother came home and told Cynthia that her father had died. The final loss of her father—just as he was coming back into her life again—was devastating to Cynthia. As she noted in her autobiography, *But I'll Be Back Again*, "It is hard to lose someone, even harder to lose him twice, and beyond description to lose him without a goodbye either time."[6]

Seeds for Change

When Robert Kennedy was assassinated the following year, it hurt Cynthia deeply. She had chosen Senator Kennedy as a hero when he began his presidential campaign. Cynthia had even received a smile and a handshake from him when she attended a campaign stop at a nearby airport.

Cynthia had seen something in Robert Kennedy that showed her that there was a larger world around her. Although she had lived her childhood contentedly in Appalachia, she began to feel a longing for something bigger. These seeds of longing were planted even more deeply in Cynthia when the New Orleans Symphony Orchestra gave a concert in the Shady Spring Junior High School gymnasium. "The gym was transformed into a place of wonder for me,"[7] Cynthia remembers of the concert. "Watching the conductor and his beautiful orchestra, I felt something in me that wanted more than I had. Wanted to walk among musicians and artists and writers."[8] There was a world outside of Beaver, and Cynthia began to want to be part of it.

However, this discontent proved difficult. Cynthia had visited big cities such as Charleston, West Virginia's capital. The tall buildings and rush of people had left her feeling small and unimportant. She felt even smaller as she began to realize that the rest of the world viewed the people of Appalachia as poor and uneducated, sometimes referring to them as "hillbillies." Cynthia's feelings of inferiority, and her self-consciousness about the way she spoke and lack of cultural knowledge would follow her all the way into adulthood.

Moving into her high school years, Cynthia stayed within her comfort zone in Beaver. She was an award-winning majorette in the school band. She participated in school plays and the student council, and she read lots of cheap romance novels. At sixteen years old, Cynthia had a steady boyfriend named Eddie. "Like most small-town girls," Cynthia remembers, "I planned to marry my high school sweetheart as soon as I graduated and looked forward to buying a nice mobile home we could live in and to making lasagna every Sunday. I didn't know how to want anything else."[9]

Cynthia's heart was broken, however, when Eddie left her for someone else. There was a reunion, and then another breakup, this time permanent. When Cynthia graduated from Shady Spring High School in 1972, her life was in transition and she had no boyfriend and no plans for her future.

3 A Love for Literature

Because her father had been in the military, Rylant was eligible for free college tuition through a Veterans Administration grant. Nobody had really encouraged her to go to college, and Rylant herself did not feel a strong drive to attend. But because she no longer had plans to marry and wasn't sure what else to do with her life, she decided to enroll. Her plan was to become a nurse, like her mother. Rylant enrolled in nursing school in Parkersburg, West Virginia.

During her first semester in nursing school, she took a variety of required courses, including freshman English 101. It was this English class that would change her direction in life. There, she was introduced to classic literature, which she loved. When she read a story by Langston Hughes, an influential African American poet and writer during the Harlem Renaissance, Rylant remembers being just knocked off her feet. She knew that literature was what she wanted to study. At the end of the semester, Rylant switched her major to English and enrolled at Morris Harvey College in Charleston (which would later become the University of Charleston).

Rylant chose Morris Harvey College thinking she would feel at home with other West Virginians. However, she found that many of the students there were from out of state. She felt very intimidated by these more "worldly" students but soon came out of her shell and made friends. She came to enjoy the variety of ideas her friends had. She also enjoyed editing the campus newspaper and being part of 4 AM popcorn parties in her dormitory.

In her classes, Rylant found that she excelled at understanding and interpreting what she read. And she became even more fascinated with literature. "The first writer I fell in love with was James Agee,"[1] she remembers. "A boy in college gave me this piece of writing in a parked car, outside my dormitory, at night in the rain. It was a mimeograph handout from a literature class. Fuzzy blue ink, cheap paper, the edges moist from the boy's hands . . . I read Agee and swallowed back my heart in my throat a hundred times as I read."[2]

Many of Rylant's classmates wanted to be writers and were inspired by the well-written literature they studied. She, on the other hand, felt intimidated as a writer after reading such gifted authors as James Agee. She felt that since she couldn't write as well as Agee, she shouldn't try. Though she had won two awards for essays she'd written in high school, she didn't consider herself a writer. Rylant assumed that writers came from privileged upper-class backgrounds. For the same reasons she had felt insecure in big cities and inferior around people she considered more worldly, she felt that being from Appalachia put her in a world far removed from the world of writers.

Rylant pursued her major in English with the goal of becoming an English teacher. She liked what she was doing so much that after she graduated with a bachelor of arts from Morris Harvey College in 1975, she enrolled in a master's program in English at Marshall University in Huntington, West Virginia. She remembers her first year of graduate school fondly. She had a small apartment in an old house and met other graduate students who introduced her to new arty ideas. Rylant became involved in "Save the Whale" campaigns, became a vegetarian, listened to classical music, hung out with her new friends, and went to class. Describing those times, she says, "I loved literature so much and every day all I had to do was attend class and listen to it and talk about it and write about it. Like a chocolate lover at a Hershey's factory, I was completely content."[3]

Real Life

When she graduated in 1976 with her master of arts in English, Rylant looked for a job as an English teacher. However, the economy wasn't very strong and there were no jobs to be found. She worked part-time at the university but was barely making enough to live on. Her mother, then living in Florida, offered as much help as she could, but Rylant wanted to make it on her own. She dreamed of a life in which she owned a home with a picket fence and two cats in the yard.

It was during this year that she met a young man who shared her dream for a more stable life. Kevin Dolin also shared her love of literature, taught classical guitar, and was studying to be a carpenter. He and Cynthia fell in love and, in 1977, got married. They got the two cats they'd both wanted, though they didn't get the house. Rylant continued to look for a job in her field. In the meantime, she worked as a waitress in a Jewish deli in Huntington.

The Children's Room

It was at the advice of a friend that Rylant applied for a job at the Cabell County Public Library in Huntington. At least she could read there, the friend had said. Though Rylant had used university libraries at college, unbelievably, she had never been to a public library. However, she thought the idea was a good one. As she recalls, "the idea of working in this old Carnegie library in Huntington charmed me and I went in and asked for a job,"[4] She got the job and worked as a clerk, checking out and shelving reels of films. "I got bored in films after awhile," she remembers. "So I asked for a change. I asked if I could work in the children's department in the basement."[5] Rylant immediately felt at home in the children's room, which was decorated with hanging medals, a fish tank, and a hedgehog in a cage.

Rylant had read so few children's books that she was amazed by the collection. As she worked shelving the books, she began to read them. She took home bags filled with books, including E. B. White's *Charlotte's Web* (1952), Virginia Lee Burton's *The Little House* (1942), and Robert McCloskey's *Make Way for Ducklings* (1941). These were the books she'd never read as a child, but she read them now, night after night. Looking back, Rylant says, "I began to feel inside me the music these writers were making. I read them and I learned."[6] And she fell in love with them. "It was Randall Jarrell's *The Animal Family* [1965] which changed me," she says. "Truly. Having read it, I could not want anything but to write as beautifully as that."[7] "And I knew," Rylant says, "with a certainty like I'd never had about anything before, that I wanted to write children's books. And I believed I would be good at it. I wasn't afraid of it."[8]

Rylant didn't tell anyone that she was trying to become a writer. She bought a good typewriter, some postage stamps, and a book called *The Writer's Market*, which listed publishers and their addresses. She circled the names of publishers where she could send completed manuscripts, and she began to write.

Exciting Changes

Writing was not the only exciting change taking place in Rylant's life. She left her job at the library only five months later, when her son was born. Cynthia and Kevin named him after one of their favorite writers, Nathaniel Hawthorne (Nate for short). Nate kept Rylant busy with frequent feedings and long wakeful nights. But between feedings and when Nate was sleeping, Rylant picked up her pen and tried to write. Her first attempts were fantasy stories, which she later described as being no good. It was reading Donald Hall's picture book *The Ox-Cart Man* (1979) that introduced Rylant to a new approach to her writing. Hall's story was about a New England farmer and his family. It was written in a heartfelt, lyrical voice, describing the simple details of the farmer's life. Instead of trying to make up fantastical stories, Rylant began to write from her heart, looking at the details of her own life.

One evening when Nate was six months old, Rylant put him to bed and lay down in her own bed with a pen and some lined yellow notebook paper, ready to write. On the paper, she wrote the words, "When I was young in the mountains." She kept on writing, and in an hour, when she was done, the piece was filled with childhood memories. "I knew it was good," she remembers. "I knew I had written something very fine . . ."[9] She typed it up, selected a publisher, and wrote a cover letter that said, simply, "Dear Editor, I hope you like this book."[10] Then, she sent it off.

About two months later, Rylant received a letter from an editor at E. P. Dutton publishers in New York City. The editor told her that she had loved her story and wanted to publish it. "I was standing in my yard when I read her letter," Rylant remembers, "and I was so excited that I yelled to the mailman, who was about four houses down, that I was going to be published! He gave me a big smile and yelled back, 'CONGRATULATIONS!'"[11]

4 Mining Stories from the Mountains

As she wrote her first published book, which she titled *When I Was Young in the Mountains*, Rylant discovered the simple, lyrical voice which she would use in her writing from this time on. Possibly, she was thinking of her grandfather, who had recently died of black lung disease, and the simple, direct way in which he had spoken, or of the love she had felt from her grandparents and the beauty of their mountain home. Maybe it was because of this that she chose Rylant, her grandparents' last name, as the name by which she would be known as a writer. She would soon come to realize how many rich stories there were from her childhood in Appalachia. She only had to mine them, as her grandfather had mined coal from those mountains to make his living.

On Her Own

While her writing career was in its beginning stages, Rylant began to have second thoughts about her marriage. "We wanted different things and were unhappy together,"[1] she reflects. In 1980, after three years of marriage, twenty-six-year-old Cynthia and her husband, Kevin, decided to part ways. Rylant had been working part-time as an English instructor at Marshall University, but this job and her small advance from the sale of *When I Was Young in the Mountains* were not enough to support herself and two-year-old Nate. On her own with a child to support, as her mother had been many years before, Rylant knew she needed a profitable career. She decided to become a librarian.

She and Nate moved to Kent, Ohio, where she would study to earn her master's degree in library science at Kent State University. Rylant remembers arriving in Kent in 1981, ". . . pulling a U-Haul trailer into a parking lot at [the] university, unloading a sleepy two-year-old from the front seat of the car, and carrying what few belongings [she] owned into a tiny student apartment with concrete floors, cinderblock walls, lumpy beds and cockroaches. Believe it or not," she says, "I adored this little apartment."[2]

Although she was busy juggling classes and schoolwork and caring for Nate, Rylant continued to write. Her next book, which would be published by Dutton as well, was a picture book called *Miss Maggie*. The story was based on an elderly neighbor of her grandparents called Miss Maggie, who lived in a dark, run-down log cabin rumored to have snakes.

Waiting and Awards

Rylant waited two years for the publication of *When I Was Young in the Mountains* and was not pleased when the publisher finally showed her the illustrations. The illustrator, Diane Goode, had dressed the book's main character in a tent-like dress, quite unlike the clothing Rylant used to wear as a child. And the illustration of her grandfather returning from the coal mines showed only his hat covered with coal dust. Her grandfather would return covered head to foot with coal dust, which was implied in the text that stated that only his lips were clean. Rylant complained to the publisher, and while Goode did not change the main character's clothing, she did change the picture of the grandfather so that he was covered head to foot with coal dust.

When *When I Was Young in the Mountains* came out, Diane Goode's illustrations won a Caldecott Honor Award, given to the best-illustrated picture books each year. The book was also a finalist for the 1982 American Book Award and honored as an American Library Association (ALA) Notable Book. Rylant's first book was a success, catching the attention of parents, critics, and children. Reviewers praised Rylant's storytelling ability and her poetic descriptions of her childhood.

Thinking toward the future, when Thomas DiGrazia was chosen to illustrate her next picture book, *Miss Maggie,* Rylant sent him a photograph of the real Miss Maggie's log cabin to help him create realistic illustrations. When the book came out in 1983, reviews were positive. A reviewer in *Booklist* stated, "This sensitive picture-book story benefits from DiGrazia's perceptive soft-focus illustrations . . ."[3]

Richard Jackson

Rylant's next manuscript, *The Relatives Came,* a bubbling recollection of her relatives' summer visits to Cool Ridge, was rejected by Dutton. Rylant sent it to other publishers, and an editor named Richard Jackson at Bradbury Press in New York City offered to publish it. Rylant and Jackson could not agree on an illustrator and Jackson decided to hold on to the manuscript until the right illustrator came along.

Richard Jackson believed in Cynthia Rylant as a writer. "Hers is a fantastically honest voice,"[4] Jackson said. However, Rylant still doubted her ability to write and didn't consider herself a writer. Jackson gave her much needed support and attention. Looking back, Rylant admits, "I thought the first couple of books were flukes and that I probably could never do one again. I don't know if I would have continued if I hadn't found Dick Jackson."[5]

After earning her master's in library science from Kent State in 1982, Rylant found a job as a librarian at the Cincinnati Public Library. She and Nate moved to Cincinnati, Ohio. Rylant describes this time of her life—where she worked to support herself and her son in a new city—as a bleak period. Even with her job, money was very tight. The publication of *When I Was Young in the Mountains* in 1982 and the knowledge that *Miss*

Maggie would be coming out the next year kept her going. Richard Jackson's support, in the form of friendly phone calls and interest in her life, her reading, and her writing, helped, too.

Back to Kent

Rylant stayed at her job with the Cincinnati Public Library for only five months. Three days before Christmas 1982, she and Nate moved back to Kent. She had only seven dollars in her pocket. Rylant got a job as a children's librarian at the Akron Public Library. During the seven months she worked there, she and Nate settled back into life in the familiar town.

Rylant reunited with old friends and met new ones. One of the people she met was a professor at the University of Akron named Gerard. He had been previously married also, and he and Rylant began to date. Both agreed that they wanted to try marriage again. They got married and lived together in a comfortable home, decorated with Gerard's whale memorabilia and prints of illustrations from Rylant's books. Gerard, Cynthia, and Nate all loved animals, and their home was filled with many pets.

Rylant developed another important friendship when Diane Ward, a children's librarian who loved her books, asked Rylant to visit her library in Monongalia County, West Virginia, and speak with the children there. Rylant accepted her offer. After the speaking engagement, Cynthia had dinner at Diane's home. The two became great friends.

Feeling more settled in her life, Rylant began to write again. She developed an awareness of the feeling she got when she was ready to write. It was like an itch, which came only occasionally, but when it did, the words came quickly. Rylant sent Richard Jackson what she wrote.

Waiting to Waltz

Besides stories, Rylant found herself writing poetry. In her college days, she had never connected with the lofty style of the poetry she'd studied. However, a book called *Paper Boy* (1979, by David Huddle), which she'd found while browsing in a bookstore at that time, had changed the way she felt about poetry. The poems were written as simple accounts of everyday life in the voice of a paperboy from rural Appalachia. Rylant had bought the book and read all the poems.

Many years later, on Mother's Day 1983, Rylant felt the familiar itch to write. She sat down in a lawn chair in her yard and wrote sixteen poems, each about her childhood and early teenage years in Beaver, West Virginia. Like the poems in *Paper Boy*, her poems were simple accounts of everyday life. The next day, Rylant wrote seven more poems, and the day after that a few more. Choosing simple words, Rylant created vivid snapshots of the people and places she'd known in Beaver. She wrote about a homeless man who sat by Beaver Creek, eccentric neighbors, and Sam, the talkative man who owned the shoe shop where Rylant and her friends often visited. After typing up twenty-nine poems in all, she sent them to Richard Jackson. He accepted them but wanted an even thirty poems for the collection.

Rylant knew right away what she must write about in her last poem. It was a subject she'd been avoiding for years. She wrote the last poem about her father. It was entitled "Forgotten," and spoke simply and deeply about the day she found out her father had died:

Mom came home one day
and said my father had died.
Her eyes all red.
Crying for some stranger.
Couldn't think of anything to do,
so I walked around Beaver

telling the kids
and feeling important.
Nobody else's dad had died.
But then
nobody else's dad had worn
red-striped pajamas
and nobody else's dad had made
stuffed animals talk
and nobody else's dad had gone away
nine years ago.
Nobody else's dad had been so loved
by a four-year-old.
And so forgotten by one
now
thirteen.[6]

Richard Jackson asked illustrator Stephen Gammell to create illustrations for the group of poems, which Rylant titled *Waiting to Waltz: A Childhood*. The collection was published in 1984 with much critical success. It was selected as an ALA Notable Children's Book and one of *School Library Journal*'s Best Books.

Rylant liked Gammell's illustrations for *Waiting to Waltz* and recommended to Jackson that Gammell illustrate her next book, *The Relatives Came*. Gammell reviewed the manuscript, and although he called Rylant and told her that the manuscript made him think of aliens coming, instead of relatives, he agreed to illustrate the book. He included likenesses of his own family members and Rylant's in the illustrations. *The Relatives Came* was published in 1985 to huge acclaim. It was selected as a *Horn Book* Honor Book, an ALA Notable Book, and a winner of the 1986 Caldecott Honor Award.

More Stories

Rylant's next project was a collection of short stories called *Every Living Thing*. As animals had always been a central part of her life—her first dog, Sissy; the chickens, dogs, and cats in Cool Ridge; the many pets she and Nate had loved—it is not surprising that they made their way into her writing. "Animals bring out the truth in people," Rylant has said. "You can see what's inside a person by the way they talk to their animals . . . So I use animals to show what my characters are about."[7]

Every Living Thing was published in 1985. Rylant dedicated the book to her husband, Gerard, stating, "For Gerry and all the living things we have loved."[8] Each story is about how an animal changed a person's life for the better. The characters in the stories range from a retired teacher whose new dog eases her back into a more active life, to a mentally disabled child who finds a turtle, who is slow, just like he is. Though the pieces were written in a simple manner, many focused on sophisticated themes, such as loneliness and isolation. Because of this, the collection was recommended for older readers. A reviewer in *Kirkus Reviews* said, "The emotions these stories convey are not simplistic or treacly [syrupy, or overly sweet], but instead are direct and powerful, an impressive feat. Rylant has another winner on her hands."[9]

Richard Jackson had also been encouraging Rylant, as he had with many authors he published, to write longer, more complex pieces such as novels, for older children. Rylant was intimidated by the idea of writing a novel. They were so long and complicated, she thought. Instead, she wrote a series of short stories, each about one character in the struggling family of a West Virginian coal miner. The main character, eleven-year-old Ellie, was based on Rylant's best friend in Cool Ridge, Cindy Mills, from her fair hair to the rotting teeth that she covered shyly with her hand when she laughed. Ellie, surrounded by her teenage sisters, is apprehensive about growing up. More than anything, she longs for the respect and love of her alcoholic father. The book focuses on Ellie's relationships with her father and her friends. Many of the incidents—such as when Ellie receives her first kiss—were based on events in Rylant's life. Rylant wrote each chapter in one sitting. When the stories were done, Richard Jackson helped her put them together to become her first novel, *A Blue-Eyed Daisy*.

When the novel came out in 1985, it was selected as an ALA Notable Book and a Child Study Association of America Children's Book of the Year. Reviewers praised the way Rylant developed her characters, showing in simple, elegant prose the way they lived their lives and endured hardships. The reviews, however, were not all positive. About *Blue-Eyed Daisy*, a reviewer in *Booklist* said that, "Though there is little plot, there is undeniable punch."[10] Rylant's books had received comments in the past from reviewers who felt that her plots lacked strength. With Rylant's focus on characters and setting, her stories were not always action-packed. Rylant explains the reasons for this focus in her writing.

> When I write I try to center down gut-level and put words to feelings farther than toward descriptive or action-filled passages. It is the interior I'm most interested in, and the poetry of the simple things.[11]

However, seeing bad reviews of her books, or even a negative comment in a good review, bothered her a lot; sometimes, it would make her cry. Because she disliked being this vulnerable to the opinions of others, Rylant asked her publishers not to show her any reviews of her books, even if they were good. She preferred to focus her energy on the creation of new work.

5 Finding Home

In 1985, with *The Relatives Came*, *Every Living Thing*, and *A Blue-Eyed Daisy* just out, Rylant felt that she was earning enough income from her book royalties to quit the part-time job she'd held for two years teaching English at the University of Akron. She wanted to concentrate on writing full-time. Rylant was also being asked by schools and libraries around the United States to visit and speak with her fans. She traveled to many places and enjoyed talking with kids about her books. However, she found that being the center of attention at these events left her exhausted and emotionally drained. Her shyness made her a nervous performer, and long days of travel were too much for her. After a while, Rylant stopped visiting schools. She felt much more comfortable at home, close to her family and pets.

A Full-Time Writer

It was around this time, when Nate was seven years old, that Rylant began writing the Henry and Mudge stories, books for beginning readers for which she would become very well known. Mudge was inspired by a huge, friendly, drooling English mastiff who belonged to Gerard. Henry was based closely on Nate, whose interests included playing with dogs, reading comic books, and eating popsicles. The first two Henry and Mudge stories were published in 1987. To date, Rylant has written more than thirty Henry and Mudge stories.

A Fine White Dust

At Richard Jackson's urging, Rylant had begun work on another novel. *A Fine White Dust* (1986) tells the story of a seventh-grader named Pete who becomes fascinated by a charismatic traveling preacher named James Carson who visits his small southern town. As with Rylant's other books, this complex novel explores family relationships and friendships, adding religion into the mix as well. Pete's budding relationship with Reverend Carson along with his growing religious convictions create tension between him and his parents and best friend, who are not church-goers. Carson takes advantage of Pete's deep religious feelings and tries to pull him away from his family and his best friend. The book explores Pete's feelings as he struggles to choose whether or not to stay or go when Carson invites Pete to leave home and travel with him.

Though Rylant wanted to focus her writing on the unconditional love Pete sought from Reverend Carson and his parents, the book also plays on the importance of religion in Pete's life. Growing up in the church-oriented Bible Belt of the South, Rylant had spent much time exploring her own feelings toward God and religion. Her fear of dying as a sinner had even led her to ask for salvation in church when she was fourteen years old. Rylant drew from these experiences and feelings as she wrote. She has noted, however, that she never felt as deeply religious as Pete, though her struggles to understand God and religion were similar.

Writing *A Fine White Dust* did not come easily for Rylant. "I got just so far along with the book and got stuck,"[1] she remembers. She had to rewrite large sections again and again. "That was the first time I felt so unconfident in my writing," she admits. "But when I finished, I felt a sense of achievement that I never felt with the other books. After I sent Dick the final two chapters, he called and said, 'You did it.' I remember my gasp, my heartbeat, and I said, 'I know, I know!' It was the first truly joyful feeling I ever had about a piece of work."[2]

A Fine White Dust was put on the *Horn Book* Honor List and it was selected as a Parent's Choice Selection of Best Books for Young Adults. In 1987, it received a prestigious Newbery Honor Award. Rylant was happily surprised by this recognition. She had worried that the religious nature of the book would generate controversy. Rylant had handled Pete's struggles with religion in an honest, direct way, though, and the book was accepted. *Booklist* called *A Fine White Dust*, "poignant and perceptive" and "one of a few but growing number of stories that unabashedly explores a religious theme."[3] Another reviewer praised Rylant for being one of the few writers who is courageous enough to explore the profound religious feelings some teenagers have. The review went on to applaud the authenticity of the main character's voice.

A New Start

Despite her professional success, Rylant had begun to feel increasingly unhappy in her marriage. It was becoming apparent that Gerard was not the person Cynthia had thought he was when she married him. She realized that she had not taken enough time to get to know him well before getting married. Instead of staying in an unhappy situation, Rylant made the decision to end the marriage.

She and Nate again made a new start for themselves. This time, though, money was less of a problem. Rylant was able to support them by lecturing part-time at the North East Ohio University College of Medicine, doing a few speaking engagements, and receiving royalties from her many books. She bought them a home in Kent, which she describes as "a sweet house," with "a front porch swing and a garden."[4] She and Nate and their pets settled in, and Rylant successfully juggled her many responsibilities. She was the mother of a growing boy who liked music and video games. She answered mail from her readers and took care of their home and pets. With good, trusted friends, such as Diane Ward, she was able to get by on her own.

Rylant occasionally attended a writers' group at Kent State University, where she met other writers. One of these writers was a man named Dav Pilkey. He had attended the university earlier as an art major. Pilkey had come back to Kent after publishing his first picture book, which he wrote and illustrated. He wanted to learn more about writing and he was studying the books he admired, including Rylant's Henry and Mudge books. When Rylant and Pilkey met, she thought that he was "the sweetest and funniest guy in the world."[5] The two of them began to spend time together.

In the meantime, Richard Jackson had moved from Bradbury Press to Orchard Books, another children's book publisher in New York City. He continued to publish Rylant's work. In 1987, Orchard published her series of short stories, *Children of Christmas: Stories for the Season* (1987), which, like *Every Living Thing*, explored themes such as loneliness and connecting with others during Christmastime.

In 1988, Orchard published Rylant's *A Kindness*, a young adult novel about a single mother and her teenage son. Anna, a painter, and Chip, her fifteen-year-old son, have a close relationship. Chip feels very possessive of his mother, and when Anna finds out that she is pregnant with the child of her New York agent, their lives are turned upside-down. The tensions between Chip and Anna come through clearly in the scenes between them as they both must come to terms with the new baby and the circumstances surrounding it. As he faces letting go of part of the closeness and possessiveness he felt towards his mother, Chip experiences struggles that are difficult and emotionally draining.

As with Rylant's other stories, she centers clearly on her characters' feelings during difficult times. She provides a close-up view of a mother-child relationship, focusing on the kindness, forgiveness, and space that each must give the other. Rylant has said that giving space and letting go have been hard for her in her own relationships, and that through this story she has been able to explore her own feelings about this difficult part of love. *A Kindness* was named an ALA Best Book for Young Adults and a *School Library Journal* Best Book of the Year. *Kirkus Reviews* called it, "A wise, beautifully crafted novel with uniquely memorable characters."[6]

An Autobiography

When Rylant had visited schools, talking with the teenage readers who read her novels, they asked her many questions about her own teenage years. Rylant hadn't been sure how to answer them. Then, she decided to write an autobiography to tell her young adult readers about those years of her life. *But I'll Be Back Again: An Album* (1989) is an honest and personal account of Rylant's childhood, with a focus on her teenage years. Rylant wrote in great detail about the people and events in her life that influenced her, including her life-changing first kiss, her maturing body, her many boyfriends, and her family. She shared a discovery she'd recently made about her father: He had written an article for an army newspaper. Rylant had never known writing had been one of his duties. "The story was about army dentists," Rylant writes, "and that's not a subject you can squeeze a lot of excitement from. But my father wrote a fine, fine article, full of life and color and intelligence, and as I read it, I realized that his voice sounded like mine. And that he had not completely left this world because the sound of him was still alive in over twenty children's books written by the daughter he left behind."[7] Finding this new connection with her father fulfilled a need for closeness with him that Rylant had had since she was four years old.

About Rylant's autobiography, a reviewer in the *Bulletin of the Center for Children's Books* wrote, "It is well written and revealing of Rylant's painful childhood . . ." and concluded by calling it "honest and heartfelt."[8]

Branching Out

Rylant continued to write prolifically, coming out with a wide variety of books. She began to work with other publishers as well as Orchard. In 1991, Harcourt Brace published her nonfiction picture book, *Appalachia: The Voices of Sleeping Birds*. This lyrical, informative essay about Appalachia was named a 1991 *Boston Globe/Horn Book* Honor Book for nonfiction.

Meanwhile, Rylant continued to work with Richard Jackson. In 1990, he published two books she'd written for young adults, *Soda Jerk* and *A Couple of Kooks and Other Stories About Love*. *Soda Jerk* is a collection of poems written from the point of view of a quiet teenage boy who works at the soda fountain at a small-town drugstore. His observations about hippies, jocks, parents, and children show insight and depth, as well as humor. *A Couple of Kooks and Other Stories About Love* is a series of short stories. The characters in these stories span a wide range of age and social backgrounds, and like in *Soda Jerk* and so many of her other works, Rylant gives a voice to those quiet people in the midst of society. In the story, "A Crush," a mentally disabled young man anonymously gives homegrown flowers to a tattooed lady he observes each Wednesday opening a hardware store. In "Certain Rainbows," a grandfather expresses his thoughts about love and life as he attends his granddaughter's wedding. In the title story, "A Couple of Kooks," two sixteen-year-olds lovingly communicate all that they think is important to the unborn baby they have conceived, knowing that they will give it away for adoption. Both books, *A Couple of Kooks* and *Soda Jerk*, were well received and named ALA Best Books for Young Adults.

In her personal life, Cynthia Rylant and Dav Pilkey continued to spend time together and soon fell in love. Rylant's confidence in marriage was not high, however, because of her two previous experiences. Instead of getting married, Dav and Cynthia were constant companions and they would help each other along in their careers. Later, Pilkey would publish his popular Captain Underpants series, based on a superhero he had created in second grade.

In 1990, Pilkey dreamt that he, Cynthia, and Nate were supposed to move to Oregon. None of them had ever been there before. Rylant decided, though, that a big change in her life was just what she needed. She had recently written in a short second autobiography for young readers, *Best Wishes* (1992), that many of her childhood dreams had come true in her life. Despite that, though, she had begun to feel down. Over the next several years, Rylant and Pilkey began to plan their move. Rylant would come to call it her "grand adventure."

Missing May

Meanwhile, Rylant had begun to work on her next book. On a recent trip to visit her family in West Virginia, she had driven by a rundown trailer by the side of a mountain. She had sensed a sadness about the trailer, somehow, and imagined an old man and a young girl living there. Rylant wondered why they were together and why they were sad. She decided they were missing someone.

The image of this trailer and the characters she'd imagined stayed with her, and she developed them into a young adult novel which she called *Missing May*. The story is told from the point of view of twelve-year-old Summer, who, like Rylant as a child, needed a home. Summer finds a family and a home in the rundown trailer with her Aunt May and Uncle Ob. Ob's character was based on Rylant's grandfather, and May's on many women in Rylant's family. When May dies, Summer and Ob must cope with their tremendous grief. Though in her grief Summer wants to be left alone with Ob, her crazy classmate, Cletus Underwood, comes visiting. In his own way, and against Summer's better judgment, Cletus turns the three of them into a family. Together, they make the journey toward overcoming grief and becoming part of life again. The strong, unique personalities of each character in this novel combine to give it life. In the following passage from *Missing May*, Rylant's lyrical, honest voice shines through as Summer explores her feelings about life and death and the pain of grieving:

> May always said we were angels before we were ever people. She said when we were

finished being people we'd go back to being angels. And we'd never feel pain again.

But what is it that makes a person want to stay here on this earth anyway, and go on suffering the most awful pain just for the sake of getting to stay?

I used to think it was because people fear death. But now I think it is because people can't bear saying goodbye.

May was lucky. When she had to say her goodbye to Ob, she had to hurt over it only once. And then she was an angel and it didn't hurt her anymore.

But Ob, Ob hurt and he kept on hurting. Living in a trailer full of May's empty spaces. Walking through May's dying garden. Sleeping in a bed that still left room for her.[9]

Rylant reflects that *Missing May* was an easy novel for her to write. The words came quickly. She recalls, "I sat down and wrote every chapter in a sitting. I thought of the words almost instantly and put them on the paper."[10] Rylant has said that she drew on her feelings of needing a home as she wrote about Summer. One wonders, also, since twelve-year-old Summer was close to the age of thirteen, when Rylant grieved over her own father's death, if Rylant drew upon those feelings of pain and loss as she wrote.

In 1992, *Missing May* was published to much acclaim. A reviewer in *Booklist* made note of the "sheer pleasure of Rylant's writing." The review also stated that while *Missing May* deals with difficult issues such as "Death, pain, and grief," Rylant writes about them "with humor, grit, and love."[11] *Missing May* would help many readers work through their own feelings and to teach and help others to cope as well, by giving them an avenue to deal with death and grieving.

One Monday morning in 1993, as the grand adventure to Oregon was coming near, Rylant received a phone call. On the line was a member of the Newbery committee, which awards the prestigious Newbery Medal each year to the children's book they vote as the best. The committee member told Rylant that *Missing May* had been selected as the 1993 Newbery Medal winner.

Rylant remembers the moments that followed the phone call as precious ones. She cried and called her mother. She later sent flowers to everyone close to her, including her best friend, Diane. Things also got busy then. Newspapers and magazines contacted Rylant asking for interviews. She obliged whenever she could. Rylant even had an invitation to appear right away on television's *Today Show*, but she declined, saying later with a laugh, "I wanted to take a nap."[12]

Winning the Newbery Medal meant many things to Rylant. She was proud that her book, with characters that represented the people she knew and loved in Appalachia, would find its way into so many readers' hands. She also felt happy for the prestige and recognition the award would bring her. Ever since *A Fine White Dust* had won the Newbery Honor, she had often been asked when she was going to win the Newbery Medal. Winning the Newbery also meant huge book sales and extra income. Rylant celebrated by buying her mother a new car and Nate a big supply of video games. She also made plans to buy children's books for the schools she'd attended as a child. For herself, she decided to buy a Steinway baby grand piano.

In June, Rylant traveled to the American Library Association's annual meeting (which was in New Orleans) to accept the Newbery Medal. In her acceptance speech, she thanked her mother, her best friend Diane, Dav, and Nate, all of whom were there with her. Rylant also voiced thanks to her grandparents, telling the audience about her years with them and saying, "There is no question in my mind that it was during those years that the writer in me was born."[13]

6 The Grand Adventure

L ater that year, Cynthia, Dav, and four-teen-year-old Nate packed up their belongings and pets and began their grand adventure. Before they said good-bye to Ohio, Rylant donated many of her original manuscripts and letters to the Kent State University library. Rylant loved the long drive that took them across the United States and she would later write a picture book called *Tulip Sees America* (1998) based on her trip.

Rylant had already bought a home in Eugene, Oregon, when she and Pilkey had flown out earlier to investigate the area. She had instantly fallen in love with a house they'd driven by and she bought it on the spot.

Pilkey bought a home, right down the street from Rylant's, surrounded by the same wooded hills.

Rylant decorated her new home with quilts, some of which she had made herself, and found a special place for her piano. She decorated the yard with flowers, stone angels, and a gargoyle, and planted a garden. In this yard, she would write many new books.

Being Bold

The grand adventure was a bold move for Rylant, who admits that normally she is "a little timid in life. Nevertheless," she counters, "I am brave in my work."[1] Rylant has always enjoyed the freedom to try new things with her writing. She has written books of many genres, including picture books, short stories, poetry, novels, and easy readers.

In another bold move in the early 1990s, Rylant began to illustrate some of her books. The first were a series of board books called *The Everyday Books* (1993), in which she experimented with construction-paper collage. Next, using acrylic paints (Pilkey recommended them because she could cover up her mistakes), she illustrated her picture book, *Dog Heaven* (1995), which she'd written in response to a sad letter written to her by Diane Ward about the death of her dog. Since then Rylant has illustrated several more of her picture books.

"Each year, I hope to be better,"[2] Rylant says about her writing, and she continues to stretch her skills. In her young adult novel *I Had Seen Castles* (1993), she tackled the difficult subject of war. The novel is told from the point of view of John Dante as he looks back at his life at age seventeen, when he made the decision to enlist in the service and fight in World War II. In love with Ginny, a beautiful girl who was strongly against the war, and close to his family, who would miss him desperately, Dante struggled with the decision to enlist, knowing he did not want to be seen as a coward. Rylant wanted to show the tension between Dante and his girlfriend that was created by this difficult decision. The book follows Dante past his eighteenth birthday as he joins the service, goes overseas, fights in the war, and returns forever changed.

Rylant did an extensive amount of research for this novel, reading memoirs written by soldiers who had fought in the war. She found it very painful to write and found, at first, that she could not write at all. She continued with it, however, and though she had never experienced war in her own life, was able to draw on what she knew was important in her life to help her connect with her character. As she explains, "The thing that I did find is that the things that matter deeply in my life, like the pleasures of just having a home . . . just the simple things like that informed the things that he missed most and lost, ultimately."[3] The book was published in 1993 and received excellent reviews.

Rylant further stretched her writing skills when she broke into the genre of fantasy. She had not done so since her fledgling attempts at age twenty-three. In 1995, her two fantasy novels, *The Van Gogh Cafe* and *Gooseberry Park*, were published. *The Van Gogh Cafe* is the story of ten-year-old Clara in Flowers, Kansas, who sees magic happen at her father's cafe. *Gooseberry Park* was an animal fantasy that included many of the animals Rylant had known in her life. It was a challenge for Rylant to make this story action-packed and fun, while giving wisdom and wit to her animal characters. However, she worked until she got it right.

Since then, Rylant has written many more books, including several new easy-reader series, including the Mr. Putter and Tabby series, the Poppleton the Pig series, and *The High-Rise Private Eyes*. Furthering her exploration of God through her writing, Rylant has written novels such as *The Heavenly Village* (1999), and recently, *God Went to Beauty School* (2003).

Writing and Life

Rylant doesn't write every day. Sometimes months go by, often in the wintertime, when she doesn't write at all. Rylant, now the acclaimed author of over 130 books, remembers her years of self-doubt, when she couldn't consider herself a "real" writer because she didn't sit in front of a computer for hours a day. Now she honors her writing process. "The creative urge strikes so unexpectedly," she explains. "I've always kept my life really quiet and simple, so that I'm ready to sit down and write or paint when it's time. You have to respect whatever it is you have to do to write, and for me, this is how I have to live."[4]

In the winter of 2003, Rylant moved to Portland, Oregon, settling into a nice home in a wooded area. Rylant's life is even quieter now that Nate is grown and living on his own, working as a composer. But, her two cats and two dogs keep her busy. And she loves to make her home a pleasant place. In fact, she rearranges her furniture so often that her friends tease her that something is different every time they visit. Rylant and Pilkey take long walks with their dogs (Cynthia rescued a stray dog and gave it to Dav), make up stories, and watch movies together. Rylant goes to the movies as often as she can, seeing the ones she likes time and again.

Rylant rarely travels, gives few interviews, and keeps the ringer on her phone turned off when she wants to be alone. To help ensure a life away from the public eye, she uses Rylant as the writing name by which she's known.

Like the quiet privacy she enjoyed when she was "young in the mountains," Rylant now spends her time quietly in the mountains of Oregon, exploring, laughing, and spending long hours working in her garden and daydreaming. When the sun is shining and she gets that itch, the feeling that it is time to write, Rylant takes her yellow pad of paper, finds a comfortable spot on the porch swing, and waits for the words to come.

Interview with Cynthia Rylant

ALICE B. McGINTY: Please describe your home and some of your favorite places there, including your favorite place to write.

CYNTHIA RYLANT: I just moved into a new house, so I'm still nest-building. It's a nice little house, with big windows, that looks out on a forest, and a garden room where the kitties love to sleep in front of the fire. I like to be in the living room with the dogs and the TV and the paper and the cookies and the tea! I like flowered chairs and white tables and lamps with little glass dangling things. But mostly, I just love my kitties and dogs. I can write anywhere.

ALICE B. McGINTY: What do you enjoy best about being a writer?

CYNTHIA RYLANT: The finished book. Getting to it has never been that exciting for me. I'd rather do lots of other stuff than write! But I'm always very happy with the finished book.

ALICE B. McGINTY: In which areas would you like to see yourself grow as a writer?

CYNTHIA RYLANT: I'd like to write more than 200 pages someday!

ALICE B. McGINTY: What are some of the things that factor into your decisions about which of your books you decide to illustrate yourself?

CYNTHIA RYLANT: I illustrated my books for a few years because I wanted to, was inspired to try. I love paint. I love it right out of the tube and slopped on to paper. I've never taken an art class. I just wanted to paint for a while, so I did. But I haven't wanted to lately. It hasn't seemed the right time.

ALICE B. McGINTY: Which of the characters in your books do you most identify with and why?

CYNTHIA RYLANT: I most admire Mr. Putter and Tabby and Mrs. Teaberry and Zeke. It seems to me that they really know how to live. I guess maybe I envy them more than I identify with them. The character I am most like is Little Owl in the Thimbleberry stories because he keeps rearranging his furniture—just like me! And I'm wild-eyed like him, too!

ALICE B. McGINTY: Why do you feel that you've been successful as a writer?

CYNTHIA RYLANT: Maybe because I try to use words that are beautiful to hear.

ALICE B. McGINTY: What would you like readers to come away with after reading your books?

CYNTHIA RYLANT: Maybe feeling satisfied and happy.

ALICE B. McGINTY: If you were not a writer, what career might you choose to pursue?

CYNTHIA RYLANT: Kindergarten teacher. Doctor.

ALICE B. McGINTY: Could you share with us any information about a current project you are working on?

CYNTHIA RYLANT: I am thinking about an old hotel and who might be in it.

ALICE B. McGINTY: What advice would you give to teenagers and young adults who are interested in writing?

CYNTHIA RYLANT: Don't overwrite. Relax. Read the good writers.

ALICE B. McGINTY: Is there a question you've been surprised that you haven't been asked in an interview?

CYNTHIA RYLANT: I don't do many interviews. No one has asked why. Here's the answer. Because I think when authors start to talk about their work, we all start to sound alike.

ALICE B. McGINTY: If you could have lunch with one of the characters from your books, who would it be, and why would you choose him or her?

CYNTHIA RYLANT: I would have lunch with Cletus because there are so few people like him. You don't have to impress Cletus. He's happy just to know you. You can talk to Cletus about anything. Hot dogs, aliens, the check-out lady at Kroger's. I used to know a lot of people like Cletus, but not anymore.

Timeline

1954 Cynthia Smith is born on June 6 in Hopewell, Virginia.

1958 Cynthia begins living with her grandparents in Cool Ridge, West Virginia, at age four.

1962 Cynthia and her mother, Leatrel, move to Beaver, West Virginia.

1967 Cynthia's father dies on June 16.

1972 Cynthia Rylant graduates from Shady Spring High School and enrolls in nursing school in Parkersburg, West Virginia.

1973 Rylant switches her major to English and enrolls at Morris Harvey College, in Charleston, West Virginia.

1975 Rylant receives her bachelor of arts degree from Morris Harvey College.

1976 Rylant receives her master of arts degree from Marshall University.

1977 Rylant marries Kevin Dolin.

1978 Rylant works as a clerk at Cabell County Public Library in Huntington, West Virginia. Rylant and Dolin's son, Nathaniel, is born.

1979 Rylant works as a part-time English instructor at Marshall University. Rylant writes *When I Was Young in the Mountains*. It is accepted by E. P. Dutton for publication.

1980 Rylant and Kevin Dolin part ways.

1982 Rylant receives her master in library science degree from Kent State University and works as a librarian at the Cincinnati Public Library.

1983 Rylant returns to Kent, Ohio, and works as a children's librarian at the Akron Public Library. *When I Was Young in the Mountains* wins the Caldecott Honor after being published in 1982.

1985 Rylant makes the decision to write full-time, and Bradbury Press publishes *The Relatives Came, A Blue-Eyed Daisy*, and *Every Living Thing*.

1991 *A Fine White Dust* wins a Newbery Honor Award. The first four Henry and Mudge books, a widely popular early-reader series, are published.

1991 Rylant publishes *I'll Be Back Again: An Album* (her autobiography).

1992 Rylant works as a part-time lecturer at the Northeast Ohio Universities College of Medicine in Rootstown, Ohio. Rylant meets author/illustrator Dav Pilkey at a writers' group. Rylant publishes *Appalachia: The Voices of Sleeping Birds*.

1993 *Missing May* wins the Newbery Medal. Rylant, Dav Pilkey, and Nathaniel move to Eugene, Oregon. Rylant publishes *I Had Seen Castles*.

2003 Rylant moves to Portland, Oregon.

Selected Reviews from *School Library Journal*

A Couple of Kooks and Other Stories About Love
1990

Ages 12 and up. Eight finely crafted stories explore various aspects of love from a variety of perspectives. From the two sixteen-year-olds, wise beyond their years, who are preparing for separation from their as yet unborn child in the title story, to the optimistic musings of an old man at his grandaughter's wedding, readers are treated to unique yet universal observations of people in love. The stories are filled with both humor and heartbreak, but the sensibility of Rylant's voice and her distinctly drawn characters evoke genuine sentiment while avoiding sentimentality. Original in plot and rich in imagery, the stories read smoothly, offering a broad range of experience and viewpoint. Although half of the stories feature adolescent characters, the themes may be of more interest to adults than to young readers. However, those who delve into the book will be well rewarded.

Every Living Thing: Stories
1985

Grade 6–9—Relationships with animals change the lives of the human characters in these twelve short stories. This framework unites a variety of plots and personalities: a retired schoolteacher acquires a "retired" dog and through her reestablishes contact with children; a pet turtle helps a "slow" boy finally gain recognition at school; a boy frightened of nuclear war is comforted by the existence of a herd of cows. These are not conventional animal stories. Rylant's deliberate, straightforward style hides a quiet intensity unusual in such short pieces. She builds plot and character simultaneously, with precisely chosen verbs and adverbs; no drawn-out descriptions are needed. A character takes a few steps, says a few words and readers know him. Although the style is not difficult to read, the tone of the stories, the basic sense of human loneliness and isolation which comes through, makes them more suitable for older readers. (One third of the stories have adult protagonists.) Besides being enjoyed for themselves, the stories would make a good classroom read-aloud, generating lots of discussion. They would also be suitable for older reluctant readers. Finely detailed, boxed pen-and-ink drawings of the animal protagonist, precede each story and express its tone.

God Went to Beauty School
2003

Ages 9–12. A collection of innovative, thought-provoking, and insightful poems. What would happen if God got a desk job? Or bought a couch at Pottery Barn? Or found some fudge in his mailbox? These are just a few of the mundane happenings Rylant places at the deity's feet. Through everyday events (like showers) to athletics (He falls twenty times while Rollerblading) to more shocking revelations (He gets arrested in a bar fight), God finds out what it is like to live like the rest of us. And guess what? He is just like one of us. He wants juice and comic books when He's sick. And through it all, God is surprised by these revelations. These short poems are visceral in their insight, and they shouldn't be considered blasphemous jokes as much as clever "what if?" ponderings. Has God just been "winging it" His whole life? Rylant has a carefully crafted response. Christian or private schools may find this collection inappropriate to their teachings, but read with an open mind and vivid imagination, it should speak to young people. A triumphant achievement.

Missing May
1992

Ages 9–12. They've been a family for half of Summer's twelve years, and when her Aunt May dies, a little bit of Summer and her uncle Ob dies too—and his whirligigs go "still as night." Ob's 'gigs are his "mysteries," works of art that capture the essence of Storms, Heaven, Fire, Love, Dreams . . . and May. For a time, he seems to be failing, and Summer fears she'll lose him, as well. Then he claims to have been visited by May's spirit. And, stranger still to Summer, he takes a liking to that "flat out lunatic," Cletus Underwood. Lunatic or no, Cletus steps unhesitatingly into the space May has left, and all three take off on a journey in search of May. It's an ill-fated journey that, nevertheless, lets Ob and Summer turn a corner in their grieving—and sets Ob free. With homely detail, Rylant plunges readers into the middle of Summer's world, creating characters certain to live long in their memories. Her tightly woven plot wastes no words; May's death and the course of her husband and niece's grieving are both reflected in and illuminated by the state of Ob's mysteries and the course of that interrupted journey of discovery. There is much to ponder here, from the meaning of life and death to the power of love. That it all succeeds is a tribute to a fine writer who brings to the task a natural grace of language, an earthly sense of humor, and a well-grounded sense of the spiritual.

Soda Jerk
1990

Ages 12 and up. In poems that stir the senses and (for older readers) the memory, an adolescent "everyman" observes his small Virginia town and reflects upon his own life from across the counter at Maywell's Drugstore in a manner reminiscent of Wilder's *Our Town*. The visual imagery in these poems is so vivid that older readers will be able to see this small town and will recognize the cross-section of those who live there. Moreover, they will see into not only this soda jerk's life but also into the lives of the jocks who "walk with their arms sticking out some five inches," the hunters for whom "a deer corpse/is cause for joy among men," and the "old ladies/who've been somebody's mom/for so long,/they have come begging/ for a person to take an interest." The first poem ends, "Tips are okay./But the secrets are better." Each poem that follows reveals the narrator's perceptions of the secrets of the people he encounters, from the sheriff to his own father. This book is one of celebration and resignation by an average adolescent who wants to impress the popular girl and watches to see if anyone buys "sexual aids," but who also cares about people in his town. Catalanotto's watercolor paintings evoke small town life without defining it too specifically and are appropriately grouped so that all but the last poem stand on stark white pages, evoking their own images. The illustrations have an old-fashioned aura, yet combined with the contemporary references in the text, the book may give readers the sense that they are caught up in a time warp rather than in nostalgic reverie.

Also, the size, format, and dust jacket indicate that this is a picture book. It will take some effort to get it into the hands of the older audience who will find themselves and their feelings captured in the poems.

List of Selected Works

Appalachia: The Voices of Sleeping Birds.
Illustrated by Barry Moser. San Diego:
Harcourt, 1991.
Best Wishes. Katonah, NY: Richard C. Owen,
1992.
A Blue-Eyed Daisy. New York: Bradbury
Press, 1985.
But I'll Be Back Again: An Album. New York:
Orchard Books, 1989.
Children of Christmas: Stories for the Season.
Illustrated by S. D. Schindler. New York:
Orchard Books, 1987.
*A Couple of Kooks: And Other Stories About
Love.* New York: Orchard Books, 1990.
Dog Heaven. Illustrated by Cynthia Rylant.
New York: Blue Sky Press, 1995.

The Everyday Books. Illustrated by Cynthia Rylant. New York: Bradbury Press, 1993.

Every Living Thing. New York: Bradbury Press, 1985.

A Fine White Dust. New York: Bradbury Press, 1986.

God Went to Beauty School. New York: Harper-Collins Children's Books, 2003.

Gooseberry Park. San Diego: Harcourt Brace, 1995.

The Heavenly Village. New York: Blue Sky Press, 1999.

Henry and Mudge: The First Book of Their Adventures. Illustrated by Sucie Stevenson. New York: Bradbury Press, 1987.

Henry and Mudge and the Happy Cat. New York: Bradbury Press, 1994.

Henry and Mudge in the Green Time. New York: Bradbury Press, 1987.

The High-Rise Private Eyes: The Case of the Climbing Cat. Illustrated by G. Brian Karas. New York: Greenwillow Books, 2000.

I Had Seen Castles. San Diego: Harcourt/ Brace, 1993.

In Aunt Lucy's Kitchen. Illustrated by Wendy Anderson Halperin. New York: Simon & Schuster, 1998.

The Islander: A Novel. New York: DK Publishing, 1998.

A Kindness. New York: Orchard Books, 1989.

Little Whistle (first of series). Illustrated by Tim Bowers. San Diego: Harcourt Brace, 2001.

Margaret, Frank, and Andy: Three Writers' Stories. San Diego: Harcourt Brace, 1996.

Miss Maggie. Illustrated by Thomas DiGrazia. New York: Dutton, 1983.

Missing May. New York: Orchard Books, 1992.

Mr. Putter & Tabby Take the Train. Illustrated by Arthur Howard. San Diego: Harcourt Brace, 1998.

Poppleton. Illustrated by Mark Teague. New York: Blue Sky Press, 1997.

The Relatives Came. Illustrated by Stephen Gammell. New York: Bradbury Press, 1985.

Soda Jerk. Illustrated by Peter Catalonotto. New York: Orchard Books, 1990.

Tulip Sees America. Illustrated by Lisa Desimini. New York: Blue Sky Press, 1998.

The Van Gogh Café. San Diego: Harcourt Brace, 1995.

When I Was Young in the Mountains. Illustrated by Diane Goode. New York: Dutton, 1982.

List of Selected Awards

***Appalachia: The Voices of Sleeping Birds* (1991)**
Boston Globe/Horn Book Award for Nonfiction (1991)

***A Blue-Eyed Daisy* (1985)**
American Library Association Notable Book (1985)
Child Study Association of America's Children's Book of the Year (1985)

***A Couple of Kooks and Other Stories About Love* (1990)**
American Library Association Best Book for Young Adults (1990)

Every Living Thing **(1985)**
School Library Journal Best Book (1985)

A Fine White Dust **(1986)**
Newbery Honor Book (1987)
Horn Book Honor List (1986)
Parents Choice Selection (1986)

A Kindness **(1988)**
Best Book for Young Adults (1988)

Missing May **(1992)**
Newbery Award (1993)
Boston Globe/Horn Book Award for Fiction (1992)

The Relatives Came **(1985)**
Caldecott Honor Book (1986)
Horn Book Honor Book (1985)
New York Times Best Illustrated Children's
    Book of the Year (1985)
American Library Association Notable
    Book (1985)
Child Study Association of America's Children's
    Book of the Year (1985)

Soda Jerk **(1990)**
American Library Association Best Book for
    Young Adults (1990)

Waiting To Waltz: A Childhood (1984)
American Library Association Notable
    Book (1984)
School Library Journal Best Book (1984)
National Council for Social Studies Best
    Book (1984)

When I Was Young in the Mountains (1982)
Caldecott Honor Book (1983)
American Library Association Notable
    Book (1983)
Horn Book Honor Book (1982)

Glossary

acclaimed Recognized or applauded.

Agee, James An award-winning novelist, screenwriter, journalist, poet, and film critic, born in Knoxville, Tennessee, who lived between 1909 and 1955. Agee's books include *Let Us Now Praise Famous Men* and *Death in the Family* (which won a Pulitzer Prize).

Appalachia A region of the eastern United States, mainly around the Appalachian Mountains, usually referring to areas characterized by large amounts of poverty and unemployment in the following states: Alabama, Georgia, Kentucky, Maryland, North Carolina, Pennsylvania, South Carolina, Tennessee, Virginia, West

Virginia, Ohio, Indiana, and New York.

Appalachian Mountains A large mountain range located in eastern North America and extending 1,600 miles from Québec to Georgia.

autobiographical Referring to someone's own life.

Bible Belt An area chiefly in the southern United States, characterized by strict and rigid religious beliefs and practices.

black lung disease A disease of the lungs mainly affecting coal miners, caused by the inhalation of coal dust. Between 1979 and 1996, 14,156 deaths were attributed to black lung disease.

Carnegie library A library that was built using funds donated by the Andrew Carnegie Foundation.

charismatic In a religious sense, an extra-ordinary grace or gift of spiritual healing.

fluke Something that happens by chance.

genres Particular kinds or categories, of literature or art.

Harlem Renaissance An artistic movement in the 1920s that celebrated black life and culture.

impeccably Flawless, free from mistakes.

Jarrell, Randall Acclaimed poet, essayist, and

critic who was born in Nashville, Tennessee, and lived from 1914 to 1965.

Korean War A war lasting from 1950 to 1953 between North Korea and South Korea, in which America sent military troops to support South Korea.

majorette A girl who marches and twirls a baton with a marching band.

manuscript The hand-written or type-written copy of a story before it is published.

memorabilia Objects valued for their connection with historical events, entertainment, or culture.

Newbery Medal An award given every year to the most distinguished contribution to American children's literature. A number of Newbery Honor Awards (usually between two and four) are also given each year to books that the Newbery committee considers to be of special merit.

phenomena Unusual, significant occurrences.

poignant Profoundly moving, touching, often bringing sadness.

prolific Producing a lot of work.

resourcefulness Being good at thinking of ways to do things.

revealing To bring into view or make known

something that was previously unknown

rural In the country or in a farming area.

salvation In a religious sense, to be saved or redeemed from sin and evil and given the chance for everlasting happiness.

treacly Overly sweet or sentimental.

unabashedly Obvious, out in the open, not concealed or disguised or embarrassed.

Veterans Administration Grant Scholarship money provided by the government to veterans of war and their families.

For More Information

Due to the changing nature of Internet links, The Rosen Publishing Group, Inc., has developed an online list of Web sites related to the subject of this book. This site is updated regularly. Please use this link to access the list:

http://www.rosenlinks.com/lab/cryl

For Further Reading

Authors and Artists for Young Adults. Volume 10. Detroit: Gale Research, 1993.

Nakamura, Joyce, ed. *Something About the Author, Autobiography Series*, Volume 13. Detroit: Gale Research, 1992.

Rylant, Cynthia. *But I'll Be Back Again: An Album*. New York: Orchard Books, 1989.

Rylant, Cynthia. *Waiting To Waltz: A Childhood*. New York: Bradbury Press, 1984.

Bibliography

Antonucci, Ron. "Rylant on Writing: A Talk With 1993 Newbery Medalist Cynthia Rylant." *School Library Journal*, May, 1993, pp. 26–29.

Berger, Laura Stanley, Ed. *Twentieth Century Children's Writers*. Fourth Edition. Detroit: St. James Press, 1995.

Burnside, Mary Wade. "Hurdling the Newbery and Moving On." *Sunday Gazette-Mail*, February 14, 1993, p. P1E.

Copeland, Jeffrey S., and Vicky L. Copeland *Speaking of Poets 2: More Interviews with Poets Who Write for Children and Young Adults*. Urbana, IL: National Council of Teachers of English, 1994.

Cooper, Ilene. "The *Booklist* Interview: Cynthia Rylant." *Booklist*, June 1–15, 1993, pp. 1,840–1,841.

Cowers, Cynthia E., and Niles Siegel. "Cynthia Rylant" (video recording). Hightstown, NJ: American School Publishers. 1990.

Cynthia Rylant Home Page. Retrieved November 10, 2002 (http://www.cynthiarylant.com).

Edwards, Eden K. Essay in *Children's Books and Their Creators*, edited by Anita Silvey. New York: Houghton Mifflin, 1995.

Frederick, Heather Vogel. "Cynthia Rylant: A Quiet and Reflective Craft." *Publishers Weekly*, July 21, 1997, pp. 178–179.

Gallo, Donald R., ed. *Speaking for Ourselves, Too: More Autobiographical Sketches by Notable Authors of Books for Young Adults*. Urbana, IL: National Council of Teachers of English, 1993.

Hedblad, Alan, ed. *Something About the Author*, Volume 112. Detroit: Gale Research, 2000.

Holmes Holtze, Sally, ed. *Sixth Book of Junior Authors and Illustrators*. New York: H. W. Wilson Co., 1989.

Julian-Goebel, Teressa. "The Voice of An Appalachian Author: Cynthia Rylant." *Ohio Reading Teacher*, Vol. 26, Fall 1991, pp. 4–10.

Keifer, Rhonda. "I'll Be Sending You Angels: A Bio-Bibliography of Cynthia Rylant." Kent, OH: Kent State University, MLS Masters Thesis, July 1993.

McElmeel, Sharron L. *The One Hundred Most Popular Picture Book Authors and Illustrators*. Englewood, CO: Libraries Unlimited, 2000.

Nakamura, Joyce, ed. *Something About the Author, Autobiography Series*, Volume 13. Detroit, MI: Gale Research, 1992.

Peacock, Nancy. "Children's Author Writes with 'Mountain Grit.'" *Akron Beacon Journal*, February 23, 1986, p. G1.

Peacock, Scot, ed. *Something About the Author*, Volume 115. Detroit: Gale Research, 2000.

"Pilkey's Web Site O' Fun." Retrieved February 12, 2003 (http://www.pilkey.com).

Rylant, Cynthia. American Book Association Speech, June 2, 1995 (rough draft/finished draft). Kent State University Special Collections and Archives, Box 1 Item 18, accessed January 24, 2003.

Rylant, Cynthia. *But I'll Be Back Again: An Album*. New York: Orchard Books, 1989.

Rylant, Cynthia. Essay. Kent State University Special Collections and Archives, Box 1 Item 11, accessed January 24, 2003.

Rylant, Cynthia. Essay in "Voices of the Creators" included in *Children's Books and Their Creators*, edited by Anita Silvey: New York, Houghton Mifflin, 1995.

Rylant, Cynthia. Indiana and Ohio Library Association Speech, September 20 and October 23, 1992. Kent State University Special Collections and Archives, Box 1 Item 16, accessed January 24, 2003.

Rylant, Cynthia. *Missing May*. New York: Orchard Books, 1992.

Rylant, Cynthia. "Newbery Medal Acceptance." *Horn Book Magazine*, July/August 1993, pp. 416–419.

Rylant, Cynthia. "Ohioana Day Acceptance." *Ohioana Quarterly*, Spring 1994, p. 9.

Rylant, Cynthia. "Thank You, Miss Evans." *Language Arts*, September 1985, pp. 460–462.

Rylant, Cynthia. *Waiting to Waltz: A Childhood*. New York: Bradbury Press, 1984.

Rylant, Cynthia. *When I Was Young in the Mountains*. New York: Dutton. 1982.

Silvey, Anita. "An Interview With Cynthia Rylant." *Horn Book Magazine*, November/December 1987, pp. 695–702.

Trumpet Club. "Cynthia Rylant" (sound recording). Holmes, PA: The Trumpet Club, 1998.

Umrigar, Thrity. "Kent's Rylant Wins Prestigious Newbery 'Missing May' Nets Writer Top Award For Children's Literature." *Akron Beacon Journal*, January 26, 1993, p. B1.

Umrigar, Thrity. "The Storyteller's Story." *Akron Beacon Journal*, October 22, 1989, p. 5.

Ward, Diane. "Cynthia Rylant." *Horn Book Magazine*, July/August 1993, pp. 420–423.

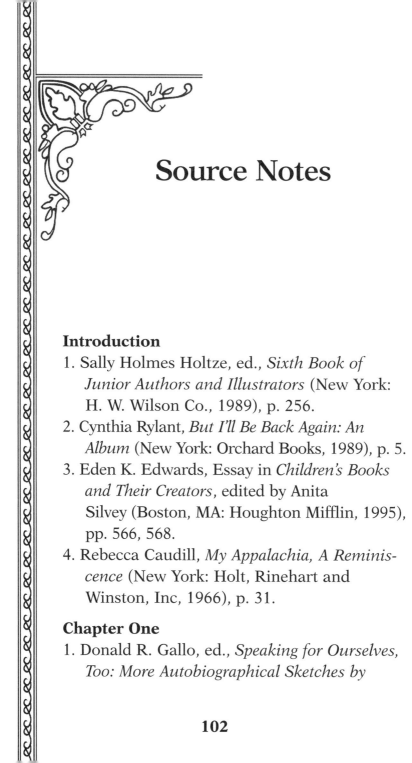

Source Notes

Introduction

1. Sally Holmes Holtze, ed., *Sixth Book of Junior Authors and Illustrators* (New York: H. W. Wilson Co., 1989), p. 256.
2. Cynthia Rylant, *But I'll Be Back Again: An Album* (New York: Orchard Books, 1989), p. 5.
3. Eden K. Edwards, Essay in *Children's Books and Their Creators*, edited by Anita Silvey (Boston, MA: Houghton Mifflin, 1995), pp. 566, 568.
4. Rebecca Caudill, *My Appalachia, A Reminiscence* (New York: Holt, Rinehart and Winston, Inc, 1966), p. 31.

Chapter One

1. Donald R. Gallo, ed., *Speaking for Ourselves, Too: More Autobiographical Sketches by*

Notable Authors of Books for Young Adults
(Urbana, IL: National Council of Teachers of
English, 1993), p. 177.

2. Cynthia Rylant, *But I'll Be Back Again: An Album*
(New York: Orchard Books, 1989), p. 8.

3. Cynthia E. Cowers, and Niles Siegel, "Cynthia
Rylant," (video recording) (Hightstown, NJ:
American School Publishers, 1990).

4. Rylant, *But I'll Be Back Again: An Album*, appendix.

5. Sally Holmes Holtze, ed., *Sixth Book of Junior
Authors and Illustrators* (New York: H. W. Wilson Co., 1989), p. 255.

6. Rylant, *When I Was Young in the Mountains*
(New York: Dutton, 1982).

7. Ibid.

Chapter Two

1. Teressa Julian-Goebel, "The Voice of An
Appalachian Author: Cynthia Rylant," *Ohio
Reading Teacher*, Vol. 26, Fall 1991, p. 6.

2. Joyce Nakamura, ed. *Something About the
Author, Autobiography Series*, Vol. 13, (Detroit,
MI: Gale Research, 1992), p. 158.

3. Cynthia Rylant, *But I'll Be Back Again: An Album*
(New York: Orchard Books, 1989), p. 38.

4. Ibid., p. 37.

5. Nakamura, p. 158.

6. Rylant, *But I'll Be Back Again: An Album*, p. 48.

7. Ibid., p. 33.

8. Ibid.

9. Cynthia Rylant, Essay (Kent State University Special Collections and Archives, Box 1 Item 11), accessed January 24, 2003, p. 3.

Chapter Three

1. Cynthia Rylant, American Book Association Speech, June 2, 1995 (Kent State University Special Collections and Archives, Box 1 Item 18), accessed January 24, 2003, p. 2.

2. Ibid., pp. 3, 4.

3. Joyce Nakamura, ed. *Something About the Author, Autobiography Series*, Vol. 13 (Detroit: Gale Research, 1992), p. 160.

4. Cynthia Rylant. Indiana and Ohio Library Association Speech, September 20 and October 23, 1992 (Kent State University Special Collections and Archives, Box 1 Item 16), accessed January 24, 2003, p. 8.

5. Ibid., p. 9.

6. Cynthia Rylant, American Book Association Speech, June 2, 1995, p. 5.

7. Cynthia Rylant, Essay (Kent State University Special Collections and Archives, Box 1 Item 11), accessed January 24, 2003, p. 3.

8. Nakamura, p. 161.

9. Mary Wade Burnside, "Hurdling the Newbery and Moving On," *Sunday Gazette-Mail*, February 14, 1993, p. P1E.

10. Thrity Umrigar, "The Storyteller's Story," *Akron Beacon Journal*, October 22, 1989, p. 5.

11. Cynthia Rylant Home Page. Retrieved November 10, 2002 (http://www.cynthiarylant.com/ writing2.htm).

Chapter 4

1. Joyce Nakamura, ed. *Something About the Author, Autobiography Series*, Vol. 13, (Detroit: Gale Research, 1992), p. 162.

2. Cynthia Rylant, "Ohioana Day Acceptance" (*Ohioana Quarterly*, Spring 1994), p. 9.

3. Denise M. Wilms, *Booklist*, May 15,1983, pp. 1,221–1,222.

4. Thrity Umrigar, "The Storyteller's Story," *Akron Beacon Journal*, October 22, 1989, p. 5.

5. Anita Silvey, "An Interview With Cynthia Rylant," *Horn Book Magazine*, November/December 1987, p. 696

6. Cynthia Rylant, *Waiting To Waltz: A Childhood.* (New York: Bradbury, 1984), p. 34.

7. Cynthia E. Cowers and Niles Siegel, "Cynthia Rylant" (video recording) (Hightstown, NJ: American School Publishers, 1990).

8. Cynthia Rylant. *Every Living Thing* (New York: Bradbury Press, 1985), dedication page.

9. *Kirkus Reviews*, October 1, 1985, pp. 1,090–1,091.

10. Denise M. Wilms, *Booklist*, June 15, 1985, p. 1,461.

11. Laura Stanley Berger, ed., *Twentieth Century Children's Writers*, Fourth Edition (Detroit: St. James Press, 1995), p. 835.

Chapter Five

1. Anita Silvey, "An Interview With Cynthia Rylant," *Horn Book Magazine*, November/December 1987, p. 699.

2. Silvey, pp. 699–700.

3. Denise M. Wilms, *Booklist*, September 1, 1986, p. 67.

4. Joyce Nakamura, ed., *Something About the Author, Autobiography Series*, Vol. 13 (Detroit: Gale Research, 1992), p. 162.

5. Cynthia Rylant Home Page. Retrieved November 10, 2002 (http://www.cynthiarylant.com/lifeNow.htm).

6. *Kirkus Reviews*, July 1, 1988, p. 978.

7. Cynthia Rylant, *But I'll Be Back Again: An Album* (New York: Orchard Books, 1989), p. 53.

8. Betsy Hearne, *Bulletin of the Center for Children's Books*, July–August 1989, p. 283.

9. Cynthia Rylant. *Missing May* (New York: Orchard Books, 1992), pp. 79, 80.

10. Ilene Cooper, "The *Booklist* Interview: Cynthia Rylant," *Booklist*, June 1–15, 1993, p. 1,840.

11. Ilene Cooper, "The Other Side of Good-bye," *Booklist*, February 15, 1992, p. 1,105.

12. Thrity Umrigar, "Kent's Rylant Wins Prestigious Newbery 'Missing May' Nets Writer Top Award For Children's Literature," *Akron Beacon Journal*, January 26, 1993, p. B1.

13. Cynthia Rylant, "Newbery Medal Acceptance," *Horn Book Magazine*, July/August 1993, p. 417.

Chapter Six

1. Cynthia Rylant. Essay in "Voices of the Creators" included in *Children's Books and Their Creators*, edited by Anita Silvey (Boston: Houghton Mifflin, 1995), p. 567.

2. Cynthia Rylant, Essay (Kent State University Special Collections and Archives, Box 1 Item 11), accessed January 24, 2003, p. 4.

3. Ron Antonucci, "Rylant on Writing: A Talk With 1993 Newbery Medalist Cynthia Rylant," *School Library Journal*, May, 1993, p. 29.

4. Heather Vogel Frederick, "Cynthia Rylant: A Quiet and Reflective Craft," *Publishers Weekly Interview*, July 21, 1997, p. 178.

Index

About the Author

Alice B. McGinty is the author of thirty-five books for children. In her nonfiction books, she has written about subjects ranging from exercise to tarantulas. Her picture books include the recently released *Ten Little Lambs* (2002, Dial Books for Young Readers). Ms. McGinty lives with her husband and two children in Urbana, Illinois.

Photo Credits

Cover and p. 2 courtesy of Scholastic.

Series Designer: Tahara Hasan;
Editor: Annie Sommers